Easy Grill Cookbook

Master the Art of Grilling with Easy and Tasty Recipes

ANTHONY TAYLOR

Your Free Gift

As a way of saying thanks for your purchase, to our readers we offer as a gift a printable recipe book, to download for free: "Cookbook Journal", a diary in which to keep track of all your culinary inventions, assigning each one an evaluation, the difficulty of execution and much more.

Click this link to free download
https://dl.bookfunnel.com/i3sq7ljm6z

Contents

Introduction

Grilling is a type of cooking that involves the application of dry heat to all sides of food, typically from the top, bottom, or sides. This method is often used to cook meat and vegetables.

Many types of grills that are available in the market, with the cheapest typically being a small $20 charcoal grill and the more expensive ones reaching $15,000. Nonetheless, the basics never change and as long as you keep practicing, your grilling skills will continue to improve as you will eventually master this practice.

There are a few rules you must observe while cooking. First, always keep the grill clean to prevent food from sticking to it. Give yourself some time before starting to cook to clean and properly heat your grill. You should also make sure to keep an eye on what you are grilling at all times and refrain from using any spray water bottle to avoid getting burned. It's also a good idea to remove any excess fat and clean your meat to decrease the amount of fat that drips into your fire.

Grills can become quite hot and easily burn your food. As such, make sure that you check the required temperature as many foods, including chicken, fish, green vegetables, and fruits, are best grilled at low temperatures.

To better control the temperature of your grill, use the dials to decrease the temperature. However, if you are using a charcoal grill, you can also test the temperature with your hands as the longer you can keep your hand over the grill, the lower the temperature is. A popular grilling misconception is that grilled items should not be turned multiple times. However, if you want to flip your food, you should, just make sure that it cooks evenly from all sides.

You should also evenly distribute the food you are cooking over the surface of the grill to decrease the likelihood of the fire flaring up. However, don't panic if this happens as it is still normal for this to take place every now and then.

Even though there are general guidelines on the amount of time it takes to grill food, it is still difficult for some people to determine when the food is completely cooked. There are a few main rules. One is that it is better to slightly overcook your food rather than undercook it, which can be dangerous, especially in the case of meat or poultry. Another rule is that you should verify that the food is fully cooked, such as by using a thermometer to check the internal temperature of the food.

The most significant advantage of having a gas grill is your ability to easily increase or decrease the temperature with a button or knob. You should also read the manual on how to use your particular grill model. For example, these are some of the basic instructions you can follow, if you have just bought a new grill:

- Uncover your grill and clean the surface. Then, turn on the gas supply.
- Wait for the grill to heat up, which should take around 10 minutes as a grill must be hot before it is used.
- Put the food on the hot grill and allow it to cook.
- Flip occasionally when needed.
- Remove the food from the heat when it's fully cooked.
- Turn off the valves.
- Once the grill has cooled down, clean the surface.
- Cover it once again and store it elsewhere.

Charcoal grilling is an art that can take some time to get accustomed to. While it doesn't cook meat or vegetables at an exactly consistent temperature, charcoal grilling can provide you with a more "authentic" experience.

As such, it is key to control the heat by creating a fire, controlling the airflow, and retaining the lid. Hence, practice is key to mastering this art. Some things you should consider while cooking over a charcoal grill are:

- Always keep your grill clean because ashes and waste can get stuck in the vents and result in poor temperature control.

- Ensure that your vents work properly as it is challenging to adjust any rusted or damaged vents.

- Wear a pair of heat-resistant gloves to prevent yourself from being burned.

- Purchase a fire starter to make a fire or use a (charcoal) chimney. Put your grill in a secure and proper position to avoid any accidents.

- Keep your grilling tools nearby, including a strong grill stick to move any burning coals.

In order to start a charcoal fire, there are a few techniques you can follow:

- Ignite the coal and then distribute it evenly.

- Wait 12 to 15 minutes for the charcoal to become hot.

- Once the charcoal is ready, it should look white or dark grey, which indicates that it is very hot from all sides.

- Scatter the charcoal and prepare a single layer of coals to have a medium-sized fire ready.

- Place two layers of charcoal in your grill if you want to attain a higher temperature.

- If you want to cook using indirect heat, then scatter the coals on one side. Then, cook your food on the other side of the grill.

Now that you know the basics of how to grill food, read on to discover how to prepare the recipes we have specified below!

COOKING CONVERSION CHART

Measurement			
CUP	ONCES	MILLILITERS	TABLESPOONS
8 cup	64 oz	1895 ml	128
6 cup	48 oz	1420 ml	96
5 cup	40 oz	1180 ml	80
4 cup	32 oz	960 ml	64
2 cup	16 oz	480 ml	32
1 cup	8 oz	240 ml	16
3/4 cup	6 oz	177 ml	12
2/3 cup	5 oz	158 ml	11
1/2 cup	4 oz	118 ml	8
3/8 cup	3 oz	90 ml	6
1/3 cup	2.5 oz	79 ml	5.5
1/4 cup	2 oz	59 ml	4
1/8 cup	1 oz	30 ml	3
1/16 cup	1/2 oz	15 ml	1

Temperature	
FAHRENHEIT	CELSIUS
100 °F	37 °C
150 °F	65 °C
200 °F	93 °C
250 °F	121 °C
300 °F	150 °C
325 °F	160 °C
350 °F	180 °C
375 °F	190 °C
400 °F	200 °C
425 °F	220 °C
450 °F	230 °C
500 °F	260 °C
525 °F	274 °C
550 °F	288 °C

Weight	
IMPERIAL	METRIC
1/2 oz	15 g
1 oz	29 g
2 oz	57 g
3 oz	85 g
4 oz	113 g
5 oz	141 g
6 oz	170 g
8 oz	227 g
10 oz	283 g
12 oz	340 g
13 oz	369 g
14 oz	397 g
15 oz	425 g
1 lb	453 g

Chapter 1: Grilled Chicken Recipes

1. Grilled Chicken Yucatan Skewers

Preparation Time: 15 min | Serving: 6 | Difficulty Level: Medium

Nutritional Info: Fat: 5g | Carbs: 2g | Protein: 14g

Ingredients

- 6 skinless and boneless chicken thighs
- ½ cup freshly squeezed orange juice
- ¼ cup lime juice
- 2 tbsp. canola oil
- 2 tbsp. ancho chili powder
- 3 cloves of roughly chopped garlic
- 2 tbsp. chipotle
- Salt and black pepper
- Chopped scallions (garnish)
- Grilled lime halves (garnish)

Steps for preparation

1. Place two skewers through each chicken thigh. Then, place the chicken in a large baking dish.

2. Whisk the orange juice, oil, chili powder, lime juice, and garlic together. Pour it onto the thighs and marinate in the refrigerator for 1 to 4 hours.

3. Heat the charcoal grill until the charcoal becomes very hot.

4. Remove the thighs from the marinade and season with salt and pepper.

5. Place the thighs over the grill. Cook them until they become golden brown and are slightly charred, for about 4 minutes per side.

6. Remove the chicken from the grill and let it rest for 5 minutes.

7. Remove the skewers from the chicken and serve with scallions and lime wedges.

2. Spicy Chicken and Grape Skewers

Preparation Time: 10 min | Servings: 4 | Difficulty Level: Easy

Nutritional Info: Fat: 6g | Carbs: 14g | Protein: 27g

Ingredients

- 2 tbsp. olive oil
- ½ tsp of lemon zest
- 1 tbsp. lemon juice
- 2 cloves of minced garlic
- 1 tsp. ground cumin
- ½ tsp. ground coriander
- ½ tsp. salt
- 1 lb. of boneless, skinless, chicken breast, cubed
- 8 wooden skewers
- 1 ½ cups seedless green grapes
- Cooking spray
- 2 tbsp. chopped mint leaves
- 1 lemon wedge

Steps for preparation

1. In a medium-sized bowl, whisk oil, lemon juice, lemon zest, garlic, cumin, salt, and coriander.

2. Add the chicken to the marinade and toss them to coat. Marinate the chicken for 20 minutes. While the chicken marinates, soak the wooden skewers in the water if they are wooden.

3. Thread four pieces of chicken and four grapes onto the skewers, alternating the pieces. Spray the grill pan with the cooking spray and preheat it to medium-high heat.

4. Grill the chicken until it is cooked through, for about 3 to 4 minutes on each side. Sprinkle some mint on top and serve with lemon wedges.

3. Chicken Sate with Ponzu Sauce

Preparation Time: 20 min | Serving: 4 | Difficulty Level: Easy

Nutritional Info: Fat: 3.5g | Carbs: 13.3g | Protein: 39.6g

Ingredients

- 4 chicken breasts
- ¼ cup light brown sugar
- ¼ cup sake (rice wine)
- ¼ cup rice vinegar
- ¼ cup fresh lime juice
- 2 tbsp. soy sauce
- 1 tsp. dark sesame oil
- ¼ tsp. crushed red pepper
- 1 minced garlic clove
- Cooking spray

Steps for preparation

1. Prepare the grill.

2. Cut both chicken breasts lengthwise into four strips. Combine the sugar and remaining ingredients in a small bowl, with the exception of the cooking spray. Then, stir until the sugar dissolves. Proceed to combine half of the mixture with all of the chicken in a large bowl and allow it to marinate for 10 minutes. Then, reserve the remaining sake mixture. Apply some cooking spray to the grill.

3. Drain the chicken and discard the leftover marinade. Then, thread one chicken strip onto a skewer and place it on the heated grill rack. Cook it for 2 minutes until done and serve with the remaining mixture.

4. Spiedini Chicken, Zucchini and Almond Salsa Verde

Preparation Time: 25 min | Serving: 6 | Difficulty Level: Medium

Nutritional Info: Fat: 5.5g | Carbs: 6.3g | Protein: 28.7g

Ingredients

- Salsa

- 1 cup chopped fresh parsley

- 2 tbsp. chopped and toasted almonds

- 2 tbsp. chopped fresh chives

- 3 tbsp. chopped capers

- ½ tsp. grated lemon rind

- 3 tbsp. fresh lemon juice

- 1 tbsp. olive oil

- ½ tsp. chopped fresh thyme

- ½ tsp. chopped fresh oregano

- ¼ tsp. kosher salt

- 1/8 tsp. ground black pepper

- 1 clove of minced garlic

Spiedini:

- 1½ lb. of chicken breasts, cut into pieces

- A small zucchini, cut into 6 slices

- Cooking spray

- ¼ tsp. kosher salt

- 1/8 tsp. black pepper

Steps for preparation

1. Soak twelve (10-inch) wooden skewers in water for 30 minutes to prevent them from burning when on the grill.

2. Preheat the grill so that it is on medium-high heat.

3. Then, to prepare the salsa, combine the first twelve ingredients and set aside.

4. To prepare the spiedini, thread the chicken and zucchini onto each of the twelve (ten-inch) skewers in alternate pieces. Coat the spiedini with the cooking spray and sprinkle salt and pepper onto the skewers. Place them on a grill rack and cook for 6 minutes or until done, turning each skewer once. Serve with salsa.

5. Grilled Watermelon and Balsamic Chicken

Preparation Time: 5 min | Serving: 3 | Difficulty Level: Easy

Nutritional Info: Fat: 12g | Carbs: 27g | Protein: 36g

Ingredients

- 1 lb. of boneless, skinless chicken breasts
- 1 tsp. salt
- ½ tsp. pepper
- 8 1-inch watermelon wedges
- 4 oz. of soft goat cheese
- 6 fresh mint leaves, finely diced
- ¼ cup balsamic vinegar

Steps for preparation

1. Pre-heat the grill. Then, season the chicken breasts with salt and pepper and cook for around 6 to 8 minutes. Add wedges of the watermelon and grill for 1 to 2 minutes on all sides.

2. Remove the chicken and watermelon from the grill. Cut the watermelon into cubes.

3. Top the chicken with watermelon, goat cheese, mint, and balsamic vinegar.

4. Serve immediately.

6. Santa Fe Grilled Chicken Soft Tacos

Preparation Time: 15 min | Serving: 8 | Difficulty Level: Medium

Nutritional Info: Fat: 5g | Carbs: 17g | Protein: 19g

Ingredients

- 2 tbsp. chili powder
- 2 tbsp. cumin
- 1 tbsp. paprika
- ½ tsp. crushed red pepper
- ¼ tsp. salt
- 1/8 tsp. pepper
- 1 tbsp. dark brown sugar
- 2 tbsp. olive oil
- 2 ½ lbs. of skinless chicken breasts

Steps for preparation

1. In a small bowl, combine the chili powder, red pepper, cumin, paprika, salt, pepper and brown sugar. Then, stir in the oil until the mixture is moist but crumbly.

2. Generously rub all sides of the chicken with the chili mixture. Let it marinate for 30 minutes at room temperature (or cover and refrigerate it for up to one day).

3. Preheat the gas grill until it is relatively hot and simultaneously preheat the broiler until it is at a high temperature. Place the rack 6 to 8 inches away from the heat source. Then, grill or broil the chicken until it is firm for about 5 minutes on each side. Let it cool for around 5 minutes and then cut it into thin strips.

4. Finally, warm the tortillas and serve them with the chicken.

7. Grilled Chicken and Tarragon-Dill

Preparation Time: 35 min | Serving: 6 | Difficulty Level: Medium

Nutritional Info: Fat: 22.1g | Carbs: 17.2g | Protein: 19.5g

Ingredients

- ½ cup lemon juice
- ¼ cup olive oil
- 4 garlic cloves, minced
- 1 tbsp. red pepper flakes, crushed
- 3 6-lb. boneless chicken breasts
- ½ cup sour cream
- ½ cup reduced-fat mayonnaise
- ¼ cup cider vinegar or rice vinegar
- ¼ cup fresh lemon juice
- 1 cup seedless red grapes
- 1 large Granny Smith apple
- ½ cup diced celery
- ½ cup finely chopped onion
- ½ cup finely chopped fresh tarragon
- 2 tbsp. fresh dill, finely chopped
- Salt and pepper to taste

Steps for preparation

1. In a mug, combine the juice of half a lemon with olive oil, minced garlic, and some red pepper flakes to form a marinade.

2. Place the chicken pieces on a plain surface and create an indentation down the middle in order to increase the surface area of each chicken breast. Then, put them in a shallow bowl, pour some olive over the chicken, and add the marinade mixture. Allow them to marinate for at least 25 minutes.

3. Mix the heavy cream, mayonnaise, mustard, and lemon juice in a small bowl to make the dressing. Mix it well and set aside.

4. Preheat your outdoor grill. Brush a bit of oil on it and put it about 4 inches away from the heat source.

5. Place the chicken on the grill, discarding any extra marinade. Grill it until the meat is cooked through, which should take roughly 4 to 5 minutes on one side. Remove it from the grill and let it cool. Slice the chicken into smaller pieces and put it in a big dish.

6. Add the apples, celery, grapes, tarragon, and dill to the chicken. Stir in the mayonnaise dressing and mix until all the ingredients are coated with the dressing. Season with some pepper and salt. Serve immediately or leave it to marinate longer overnight.

8. Grilled Lemon Chicken and Leeks

Preparation Time: 20 min | Serving: 4 | Difficulty Level: Easy

Nutritional Info: Fat: 11g | Carbs: 15g | Protein: 28g

Ingredients

- 1 tbsp. lemon zest
- 2 tbsp. fresh lemon juice
- 2 tsp. chopped rosemary
- ½ tsp. kosher salt
- ¼ tsp. black pepper
- 2 tbsp. olive oil
- 4 4-oz. chicken breasts
- 4 large leeks
- 1 tbsp. unsalted butter, cubed
- 2 garlic cloves, sliced
- 1 lemon, halved

Steps for preparation

1. Preheat your grill to about 450°F. Combine the lemon zest, salt, black pepper, lemon juice, rosemary, and 1 tablespoon of oil in a big zip-lock bag. Then, add the chicken pieces to the mixture and seal the bag. Flip the bag to coat the chicken with the marinade. Place it aside.

2. Rub half a tablespoon of oil on the leeks. Then, position the leeks over the grill and cook uncovered until grill marks appear, which should take about 7 to 8 minutes. Move the leeks to a large sheet of aluminum foil. Then, add butter and grated garlic in the foil and fold it securely.

3. Then, temporarily remove the foil from the grill and put the chicken and lemon pieces inside it, returning it to the grill. Cook the chicken fully, grilling for 2 to 4 minutes per side. Then, use some lemon juice and serve hot.

9. Chicken Pesto Kebabs

Preparation Time: 30 min | Serving: 6 | Difficulty Level: Easy

Nutritional Info: Fat: 21.3g | Carbs: 6.2g | Protein: 35g

Ingredients

- 1 cup pesto
- 1 ½ lbs. of boneless, chicken breasts pieces, cubed
- 2 pints of cherry tomatoes
- Kosher salt and black pepper (to taste)
- 2 tbsp. of chopped parsley leaves

Steps for preparation

1. In a large-sized Ziploc bag, mix the chicken with pesto, marinating it for at least 35 minutes or overnight. Drain any excess marinade and take the chicken out of the bag.

2. Thread the chicken and the cherry tomatoes onto the skewers, then season with salt and black pepper.

3. Preheat your grill until it reaches a medium-high temperature.

4. Put the skewers over the grill and flip the sides periodically until the chicken pieces are fully cooked, which should take around 12 to 15 minutes.

5. Serve hot.

10. Grilled Chicken with Balsamic Vinegar

Preparation Time: 15 min | Serving: 4 | Difficulty Level: Easy

Nutritional Info: Fat: 24g | Carbs: 7g | Protein: 42g

Ingredients

- 6 tbsp. balsamic vinegar
- 6 6-oz. skinless chicken breasts
- 2 tbsp. olive oil
- 1 garlic clove, minced
- Black pepper and salt, to taste
- 8 oz. of fresh mozzarella
- 2 large Roma tomatoes, sliced
- ¼ cup chopped basil

Steps for preparation

1. In a medium-sized saucepan, heat the balsamic vinegar over a low flame. Bring it to a boil, then decrease the heat gradually and allow it to simmer. Keep stirring regularly until the quantity has reduced to half, which should take around 12 minutes. Now, remove it from the heat and put it aside.

2. Brush the grill gently with some oil and pre-heat it until it reaches medium-high heat. In a cup, mix the olive oil with garlic.

3. Brush some oil on both sides of the chicken, further seasoning with black pepper and salt on each side.

4. Put the chicken over a grill and cover each chicken piece with slices of mozzarella and 2 or 3 slices of Roma tomatoes. Transfer to a plate and cover with aluminum foil, allowing it to rest for 7 to 10 minutes.

5. Remove the foil and brush the tops with some basil and balsamic vinegar. Finally, sprinkle some pepper on top and serve immediately.

Chapter 2: Grilled Turkey Recipes

1. Teriyaki Burgers with Grilled Pineapple

Preparation Time: 10 min | Serving: 4 | Difficulty Level: Easy

Nutritional Info: Fat: 7g | Carbs: 25g | Protein: 23g

Ingredients

For the burgers:

- 1 lb. of ground turkey
- ¼ cup breadcrumbs
- 1 tbsp. fresh garlic, minced
- 1 tbsp. fresh ginger, minced
- ½ tsp. black pepper
- ¼ cup chopped fresh cilantro
- 4 rings of canned pineapple
- 1 red onion
- Hamburger buns (serving)

For the teriyaki sauce:

- ¼ cup leftover pineapple juice
- ½ cup soy sauce
- 2 tbsp. rice vinegar
- 1 tbsp. honey
- 1 tsp. minced garlic
- 2 tsp. minced fresh ginger
- 1 tbsp. cornstarch

Steps for preparation

1. Place a small saucepan on the stove and place it on a medium-high flame. Combine all the ingredients for the teriyaki sauce with the exception of the corn starch and bring

the mixture to a boil. Remove the lid and cook it for about 1 minute, stirring constantly. In a separate small bowl, whisk the cornstarch and one tablespoon of water. Add the slurry, stir it, and keep the pan on the heat for an additional minute before removing.

2. In a large bowl, combine all the ingredients for the burgers and three tablespoons of teriyaki sauce. Then, mix everything well until it is combined. Then, shape the meat into thick patties and place in the refrigerator for about 30 minutes.

3. Preheat the grill to medium-high heat and lightly brush it with oil. Then, grill the pineapple rings and slices of red onion until they are caramelized and tender, which should take about 3 minutes per side. Proceed to grill the burgers. After flipping each patty, brush the meat with the sauce. Continue cooking until the burgers are cooked.

4. Place the burgers inside the buns, brush with sauce, and top with the grilled pineapple and red onion.

Chapter 3: Grilled Beef and Lamb Recipes

1. Skirt Steak Tacos

Preparation Time: 20 min | Serving: 4 | Difficulty Level: Easy

Nutritional Info: Fat: 19g | Carbs: 34g | Protein: 25g

Ingredients

- 1 lb. of skirt steak

- 1 tsp. salt

- ½ tsp. black pepper

- ½ tsp. ground cumin

- 2 tbsp. grated red onion

- 1 tsp. lime zest

- Grapeseed oil

- ¾ cup diced tomatoes

- ¼ cup thinly sliced radishes

- 1 tbsp. of fresh lime juice

- 1 tbsp. olive oil

- 8 6-inch corn tortillas, warmed

- 8 sprigs of torn cilantro

- 2 oz. of crumbled queso fresco

- 8 lime wedges (serving)

Steps for preparation

1. Preheat the grill until it reaches the temperature 450°F to 550°F. Then, sprinkle the steak with salt, pepper, and cumin. Rub the steak with the onion and lime zest.

2. Then, generously apply grapeseed oil to the grill grate. Proceed to grill the steak, for approximately 3 to 4 minutes per side. Make sure to cover it with the grill lid as it cooks. Then, remove the meat from the grill and let it rest for 10 minutes before thinly slicing the meat across the grain.

3. Finally, place the tomato pieces, lime juice, radishes, and olive oil in a small bowl. Mix them together. Then, divide the steak pieces evenly between the tortillas. Then, top each with some of the tomato mixture, cilantro, and cheese.

4. Serve with lime wedges.

2. Coffee Beef Tenderloin Steaks

Preparation Time: 5 min | Serving: 4 | Difficulty Level: Easy

Nutritional Info: Fat: 6.3g | Carbs: 5.8g | Protein: 22g

Ingredients

- 1 cup strong coffee
- 1½ tbsp. dark brown sugar
- ½ tsp. salt
- ½ tsp. pepper
- ¼ tsp. ground red pepper
- 2 garlic cloves, minced
- 4 4-oz. beef tenderloin steaks, trimmed
- Cooking spray

Steps for preparation

1. Combine the first six ingredients in a large zip-top bag. Then, add the steaks and seal the bag. Marinate it in the refrigerator for around 8 hours and turn the meat occasionally.

2. Preheat the grill and apply some cooking spray to it.

3. Proceed to remove the steaks from the marinade and discard the remainder of the marinade. Then, place the steaks on the grill rack, grilling the meat for two minutes on each side until it reaches the desired doneness.

4. Finally, serve with grilled asparagus and tomatoes.

3. Grilled Steak with Caper-Herb Sauce

Preparation Time: 30 min | Serving: 4 | Difficulty Level: Easy

Nutritional Info: Fat: 13g | Carbs: 2.4g | Protein: 16.3g

Ingredients

- 1 1-lb. boneless sirloin steak
- ¼ tsp. salt
- ¼ tsp. black pepper
- Cooking spray
- 1 cup parsley leaves
- 1 cup basil leaves
- 2 tbsp. green onions
- 2 tbsp. olive oil
- 2 tbsp. chicken broth
- 1 tbsp. capers
- 1 tbsp. fresh lemon juice
- 1 garlic clove, chopped
- 1 canned anchovy fillet, chopped

Steps for preparation

1. Prepare the grill until it reaches medium-high heat. Add some cooking spray to the grill rack.

2. Then, season the steak with some salt and pepper. Place the steak on the grill rack, grilling each side for 6 minutes. Then, allow it to rest for 10 minutes.

3. Place the parsley and remaining ingredients in the food processor and pulse it until it is blended. Slice the steak diagonally and serve with the sauce.

4. To prepare the garlic bread, grill four slices of French bread for 2 minutes on both sides or until they are toasted. Then, brush each slice with olive oil and minced garlic.

4. Grilled Lamb Chops

Preparation Time: 20 min | Serving: 6 | Difficulty Level: Easy

Nutritional Info: Fat: 17g | Carbs: 1g | Protein: 20g

Ingredients

- 1/3 cup olive oil
- ½ cup fresh mint leaves
- ¼ tsp. red pepper flakes
- Sea salt
- 12 small lamb chops
- 2 cloves of garlic, smashed

Steps for preparation

1. Preheat the grill to medium-high heat. Mix the olive oil, red pepper flakes, mint, and salt in a bowl. Then, rub the garlic on the lamb chops.

2. Place a few tablespoons of mint oil in a small bowl and use it to brush on the chops.

3. Grill the chops for 3 to 4 minutes per side.

4. Transfer the meat to a platter and brush the remaining mint oil on it. Sprinkle with the mint and serve with mint oil.

Chapter 4: Grilled Seafood Recipes

1. Shrimp Tacos (Chipotle with Mango Salsa)

Preparation Time: 5 min | Serving: 6 | Difficulty Level: Medium

Nutritional Info: Fat: 5g | Carbs: 21g | Protein: 16g

Ingredients

- 8 corn tortillas
- 1 lb. raw jumbo shrimp, peeled and deveined
- 1 tsp. chili powder
- ½ tsp. salt
- ½ cup chipotle sauce
- 2 cups mango salsa
- 1/3 cup Greek yogurt
- 2 tbsp. mayonnaise
- 2 tsp. lime juice
- ½ chipotle pepper
- 2 tsp. adobe sauce
- ¼ tsp. salt
- ½ tsp. garlic, finely chopped
- ½ tsp. cumin

Steps for preparation

1. Spray both sides of the corn tortillas with a non-stick spray. Then, cook the tortillas for around 30 to 45 seconds on both sides in a large skillet over medium heat. Set it aside.

2. Pat the peeled and deveined shrimp until it is dry and toss with chili powder and salt. After the tortillas are cooked, spray the pan with a non-stick spray and add shrimp to it.

3. Cook the pieces for around 3 to 4 minutes.

4. Top the tortillas with shrimp, mango salsa, and a tablespoon of chipotle sauce.

5. Serve immediately.

2. Spicy Filet Mignon with Grilled Sweet Onion

Preparation Time: 20 min | Serving: 4 | Difficulty Level: Easy

Nutritional Info: Fat: 3.7g | Carbs: 8.4g | Protein: 24.6g

Ingredients

- Cooking spray
- 2 cups Vidalia
- 1/7 tsp. of salt
- 1 tsp. garlic powder
- ½ tsp. ground cumin
- ½ tsp. dried oregano
- ¼ tsp. salt
- ¼ tsp. of ground red pepper
- ¼ tsp. black pepper
- 4 4-oz. filet mignon
- 2 small onions, sliced

Steps for preparation

1. Heat the grill pan over medium-high heat and apply some cooking spray to it. Then, add the onion slices to the pan and season with a pinch of salt and black pepper. Sauté the onions for eight minutes, stirring occasionally. Then, remove them from the pan and keep them warm.

2. Combine the garlic powder with the remaining 5 ingredients in a small bowl and rub into both sides of the beef. Then, proceed to grill the beef in the pan for 5 minutes.

3. Serve with the onion mixture.

3. Grilled Halibut

Preparation Time: 20 min | Serving: 4 | Difficulty Level: Easy

Nutritional Info: Fat: 7.8g | Carbs: 19.5g | Protein: 37g

Ingredients

- 2 cups plum tomatoes, seeded and diced
- 1½ cups ripe mango, diced and peeled
- ½ cup diced onion
- ½ cup chopped fresh cilantro
- 2 tbsp. lime juice
- 1 tbsp. cider vinegar
- 1 tsp. sugar
- 1 tsp. salt
- 1 tsp. black pepper
- 2 garlic cloves, minced
- 4 6-oz. halibut fillets
- 1 tbsp. olive oil

Steps for preparation

1. Preheat the grill.
2. Combine the first 7 ingredients. Then, stir in half a teaspoon of salt, half a teaspoon of pepper, and garlic.
3. Brush some oil on the halibut and sprinkle with a pinch of salt and pepper. Then, grill the fish for 3 minutes.
4. Serve with the mango salsa.

4. Chimichurri Shrimp

Preparation Time: 15 min | Serving: 4 | Difficulty Level: Easy

Nutritional Info: Fat: 6.5g | Carbs: 2g | Protein: 4g

Ingredients

- 1 cup arugula leaves

- ½ cup parsley leaves

- 2 tbsp. chopped shallots

- 2 tbsp. fresh lemon juice

- 2 tbsp. olive oil

- ¼ tsp. crushed red pepper

- 1 garlic clove

- ½ tsp. kosher salt

- Cooking spray

- 2 tsp. canola oil

- 1 lb. of shrimp (peeled, deveined, and with their tails)

- ½ tsp. black pepper

Steps for preparation

1. Preheat the grill to a high temperature.

2. Place the first seven ingredients and a pinch of salt in the food processor and pulse until it is blended.

3. Apply some cooking spray on the grill rack. Next, combine the oil and shrimp in the bowl and mix well. Then, thread four shrimp pieces onto each of the six skewers. Proceed to place the skewers on the grill rack for 2 minutes or until the shrimp is done cooking. Arrange the shrimp on the platter and season with salt and pepper. Then, add the sauce.

4. Serve.

5. Italian Grilled Shrimp

Preparation Time: 15 min | Serving: 4 | Difficulty Level: Easy

Nutritional Info: Fat: 20g | Carbs: 19g | Protein: 25g

Ingredients

- 2 tbsp. honey
- 3 tbsp. olive oil
- 1 ½ lb. of raw shrimp (with tails)
- Grapeseed oil
- 2 cups loosely packed arugula
- 1¼ cups chopped heirloom tomatoes
- ½ cup kalamata olives, halved
- ½ cup sliced red onion
- 1 tbsp. red wine vinegar
- ½ tsp. salt
- ½ tsp. black pepper
- 2 tbsp. fresh oregano leaves

Steps for preparation

1. Preheat the grill until it reaches a high temperature of 450°F to 550°F. Then, whisk together the honey and olive oil in a medium-sized bowl. Proceed to add the shrimp and toss it to coat.

2. Then, brush the grill grate with grapeseed oil. Grill the shrimp and cover with the grill lid until it is done, for about 1.5 minutes per side.

3. Then, toss together the tomatoes, olives, arugula, and onion pieces in the large bowl. Add some vinegar, olive oil, shrimp, salt, and pepper. Toss the contents, transfer the mixture to a platter, and sprinkle with oregano.

4. Serve it immediately.

6. Spinach Salad with Grilled Shrimp

Preparation Time: 30 min | Serving: 4 | Difficulty Level: Easy

Nutritional Info: Fat: 5.9g | Carbs: 6.9g | Protein: 24.8g

Ingredients

Dressing:

- 2 tbsp. of rice vinegar
- 2 tbsp. fresh orange juice
- 1.5 tbsp. extra virgin olive oil
- 1 tbsp. honey
- 1 tbsp. soy sauce
- ½ tsp. fresh ginger
- ½ tsp. salt
- 1/8 tsp. crushed red pepper

Shrimp:

- 2 tsp. extra virgin olive oil
- 1 tsp. fresh ginger, peeled
- ½ tsp. ground cumin
- ¼ tsp. salt
- ¼ tsp. black pepper
- 2 garlic cloves, minced
- 2 lbs. of large shrimps, peeled and deveined.
- Cooking spray

Salad:

- 8 cups baby spinach
- 2 cups shiitake mushroom caps
- ¾ cup red onion (sliced thin)

Steps for preparation

1. Preheat the grill.

2. Combine the first eight ingredients in the large bowl and stir well. Set the bowl aside.

3. Then, combine two teaspoons of olive oil and the next six ingredients in a large bowl. Mix the ingredients well and proceed to thread about five shrimp pieces onto the skewers. Place the skewers on the grill rack, which should be coated with the cooking spray. Proceed to grill them for three minutes or until they are done.

4. Add the spinach, mushrooms, and onion slices to the vinegar mixture and toss gently. Serve with the shrimp skewers.

7. Grilled Salmon with White Bean and Arugula Salad

Preparation Time: 30 min | Serving: 4 | Difficulty Level: Easy

Nutritional Info: Fat: 15.4g | Carbs: 21g | Protein: 40g

Ingredients

- 1 tbsp. chopped capers, rinsed and drained.
- ¼ tsp. grated lemon rind
- 3 tbsp. fresh lemon juice
- 2 tbsp. olive oil
- ¾ tsp. salt
- ½ tsp. fresh garlic, minced
- 1/8 tsp. ground red pepper
- 1 can of great northern beans, rinsed and drained
- Cooking spray
- 4 6-oz. salmon fillets
- ¼ tsp. black pepper
- 4 cups loosely packed arugula
- ½ cup sliced red onion

Steps for preparation

1. In a bowl, mix the capers, oil, salt, garlic, rind, juice, and red pepper together. Then, add the beans.

2. Place the grill pan over a medium-high flame. Then, apply some oil spray to the pan and the salmon. Proceed to season it with some salt and pepper before placing the salmon onto the pan, skin-side down. Cook the fish for about 6 minutes before flipping it over. Sauté the other side for 1 minute or until you're finished.

3. Add the arugula and onions to the bean dish. Add any leftover capers and divide the salad and fillets between four plates. Serve immediately.

8. Shrimp Skewers and Shashti with Chimichurri

Preparation Time: 25 min | Serving: 40 | Difficulty Level: Easy

Nutritional Info: Fat: 16g | Carbs: 5g | Protein: 24g

Ingredients

- 1 cup parsley leaves
- 1 cup cilantro leaves
- ¼ cup basil leaves
- 2 garlic cloves
- ½ tsp. grated lemon rind
- 2 tbsp. lemon juice
- ¼ tsp. red pepper (crushed)
- 4 tbsp. olive oil
- ¾ tsp. salt
- 1½ lbs. of large shrimp
- 16 Shashti peppers
- ¼ tsp. black pepper
- 2 tbsp. cooking spray

Steps for preparation

1. Preheat the grill until it reaches medium-high heat.

2. Blend the parsley, coriander, basil seeds, and garlic using a food processor to make a marinade. Add some lemon juice, red pepper, 3 tablespoons of olive oil, and a pinch of salt. Blend the mixture again until most of the contents have been roughly chopped.

3. Mix the shrimps with 1/8 cup of the mixture. Thread 4 shrimps onto 8 (6") skewers and thread 6 peppers onto the 2 (8") skewers. Then, drizzle one tablespoon of olive oil onto the

skewers. Proceed to sprinkle some black pepper and salt onto them.

4. Place the skewers on the grill and spray them with some oil. Grill them until the shrimps are done cooking and the peppers are charred, which should take about 3 to 5 minutes per side. Brush the remainder of the herb mixture over the skewers before eating.

Chapter 5: Grilled Vegetable and Fruit Recipes

1. Grilled Artichokes

Preparation Time: 15 min | Serving: 3 | Difficulty Level: Easy

Nutritional Info: Fat: 2g | Carbs: 3g | Protein: 3.2g

Ingredients

- 3 cloves of garlic

- 2 artichokes

- 2 tsp. lemon juice

- ½ cup mayonnaise

- ½ tsp. salt

Steps for preparation

1. Slice the artichokes from the top. Proceed to trim the stems and little thorns. Slice the artichoke in half.

2. In a large pot, add enough water to cover the bottom of the pot. Then, add a bit of lemon juice and garlic to the water. Bring it to a boil and add the steamer basket to the pot. Place the artichokes in the steamer basket, cover it, lower the heat, and then allow the water to simmer for around 20 to 30 minutes.

3. Mince one clove of garlic and mix it with lemon juice, mayonnaise, and salt. Set the mixture aside.

4. Use a spoon and scrape out the choke of the artichoke (the hair-like pointy fibers). Place the artichokes on a preheated grill and cook them for about 5 to 10 minutes, turning them frequently.

5. Serve immediately with a dipping sauce and enjoy.

2. Grilled Vegetables

Preparation Time: 10 min | Serving: 4 | Difficulty Level: Easy

Nutritional Info: Fat: 8g | Carbs: 7g | Protein: 3g

Ingredients

- 2 lbs. of assorted vegetables, halved
- 5 tbsp. olive oil
- 2 tbsp. lemon juice
- 1 tsp. salt
- 1/4 tsp. pepper
- 1½ dried Italian seasoning
- 1½ tsp. minced garlic
- ¼ cup parsley leaves, chopped
- Lemon wedges, optional
-

Steps for preparation

1. Combine the lemon juice, olive oil, salt, pepper, seasoning, and minced garlic in a large bowl. Then, whisk everything together.

2. Add the vegetables to the bowl and mix them until they are coated with the vinaigrette. Cover and refrigerate the bowl for 20 minutes or 2 hours.

3. Preheat the grill to medium-high heat.

4. Add denser vegetables, such as carrots. Cook them for 3 to 4 minutes and then add the rest of the vegetables to the grill.

5. Cook the vegetables for around 3 to 5 minutes per side.

6. Place the vegetables on the serving plate. Then, sprinkle with the parsley and garnish with the lemon wedges.

3. Grilled Pineapple

Preparation Time: 25 min | Serving: 4 | Difficulty Level: Easy

Nutritional Info: Fat: 3g | Carbs: 12g | Protein: 0.3g

Ingredients

- 2 tbsp. honey
- 1 tsp. olive oil
- 1 tbsp. fresh lime juice
- 1 tsp of ground cinnamon
- 8 pineapples, sliced into ½-inch thick pieces

Steps for preparation

1. In a small bowl, whisk together the honey, lime juice, olive oil, and cinnamon. Set the bowl aside.

2. Heat a grill pan and coat it with cooking spray.

3. Brush some of the marinade onto the pineapple.

4. Grill the pineapple until it is tender and golden, for about 3 to 4 minutes on each side.

5. Serve warm.

4. Pasta and Grilled Vegetables with Goat Cheese

Preparation Time: 20 min | Serving: 4 | Difficulty Level: Easy

Nutritional Info: Fat: 5.5g | Carbs: 56.3g | Protein: 14g

Ingredients

- 1 large zucchini
- 1 red bell pepper
- 1 leek, trimmed and halved
- 1 can of artichoke hearts
- 1 radicchio, quartered
- ½ tsp of salt
- ¼ tsp. black pepper
- 2 garlic cloves, minced
- Cooking spray
- 4 cups cooked Rotini
- 1 cup grape/cherry tomatoes
- ¾ cup crumbled goat cheese
- 2 tbsp. chopped fresh basil

Steps for preparation

1. Preheat the grill.

2. Place the zucchini, leek, bell pepper, artichokes, and radicchio in a single layer in a pan. Sprinkle some salt, black pepper, and garlic on top of the vegetables. Then, lightly coat the vegetables with cooking spray. Place the vegetables on the grill rack and allow them to cook for 3 minutes on all sides or until they are browned and tender. Remove the vegetables from the grill and place on a cutting board. Chop them into bite-sized pieces.

3. Place the pasta in a large bowl and season with the remaining salt. Toss well and stir in the grilled vegetables and tomatoes. Proceed to add the cheese and basil, before stirring once again.

4. Serve.

5. Grilled Okra and Tomato Skewers

Preparation Time: 25 min | Serving: 8 | Difficulty Level: Medium

Nutritional Info: Fat: 2.4g | Carbs: 5.5g | Protein: 1.3g

Ingredients

- 2 small onions, cut into 8 wedges
- 24 okra pods, trimmed
- 16 cherry tomatoes
- 4 tsp. olive oil
- 1 tsp. kosher salt
- 1 tsp. black pepper
- 1 tsp. water
- ½ tsp. ground red pepper
- 1/8 tsp. sugar
- 2 garlic cloves, minced
- Cooking spray

Steps for preparation

1. Preheat the grill.

2. Divide the onion wedges into two equal pieces. Then, thread three okra pods, two cherry tomatoes, and two onion pieces consecutively onto each of the 8 skewers.

3. Combine the olive oil, kosher salt, and remaining ingredients, with the exception of the cooking spray. Stir everything together.

4. Coat the grill rack with some cooking spray.

5. Brush the olive oil mixture onto the skewers and place them on the grill rack, cooking them for three minutes on each side or until tender.

6. Grilled Eggplant and Tomato Sandwiches with the Roquefort Dressing

Preparation Time: 15 min | Serving: 2 | Difficulty Level: Easy

Nutritional Info: Fat: 8.4g | Carbs: 42.6g | Protein: 9g

Ingredients

- ¼ cup plain yogurt
- 3 tbsp. crumbled Roquefort
- 2 tbsp. fresh parsley, minced
- 1 tbsp. light mayonnaise
- 1 garlic clove, minced
- 2 Japanese eggplants
- Cooking spray
- 8 slices of ciabatta bread
- 8 slices of tomato
- ¼ tsp of salt
- ¼ tsp. black pepper
- 2 cups trimmed arugula

Steps for preparation

1. Preheat the grill.
2. Combine the first five ingredients in the small bowl and stir everything.
3. Remove the stems of the eggplants and proceed to cut each lengthwise. Lightly coat the eggplant halves as well as the grill rack with cooking spray. Then, place the eggplant on the rack and grill it for 3 minutes on each sides. Remove it from the grill and cut the eggplant pieces into slices. Place the bread slices on the grill rack and toast them for 3 minutes on each side.
4. Spread the yogurt mixture onto each of the four toast slices. Then, top each of them with three eggplant pieces and two tomato

slices. Season with salt and pepper. Top the tomato slices with 1/2 a cup of arugula and cover with the remaining toast slices.

7. Grilled Broccoli with Lemon and Farro over Hummus

Preparation Time: 20 min | Serving: 6 | Difficulty Level: Easy

Nutritional Info: Fat: 4g | Carbs: 54g | Protein: 14g

Ingredients

- 1 cup uncooked Italian farro
- 2 lbs. of broccoli (3 large heads, cut into florets)
- 10 tbsp. olive oil
- ¼ tsp. black pepper
- 1¼ tsp. salt
- 2 quartered and seeded lemons
- 3 pieces of pita bread
- ¼ cup fresh cilantro, chopped
- ½ tsp. granulated sugar
- 1 container of hummus

Steps for preparation

1. Place a pot of water on high heat and wait for it to boil. Add the uncooked farro and lower the heat. Allow it to simmer for about 20 minutes until the farro becomes tender. Then, drain it.

2. While the farro cooks, preheat the grill until it reaches a temperature of 500°F. Apply some cooking spray to the grill. Then, mix the broccoli, oil, pepper, and salt in a large bowl.

3. Place the broccoli and lemons on the grates of the grill and keep it there until the broccoli starts to char, for around 2 to 3 minutes per side. Then, remove it from the grill.

4. Brush the pita bread with oil and toast lightly for about 1.5 minutes per side. Remove from the grill and cut into quarters.

5. Serve.

8. Grilled Pineapple Served with Toasted Coconut

Preparation Time: 20 min | Serving: 6 | Difficulty Level: Easy

Nutritional Info: Fat: 4g | Carbs: 0.9g | Protein: 2g

Ingredients

- 1/3 cup honey
- 3 tbsp. fresh lime juice
- 2 tbsp. unsalted butter, melted
- ¼ tsp. salt
- 2 3-lb. fresh pineapples, cored and quartered lengthwise
- 1 cup salted coconut chips

Steps for preparation

1. Preheat the grill to a high temperature of 500°F. Mix the honey, lime juice, butter, and salt in a small bowl.

2. Brush a quarter of the honey mixture on the pineapple pieces and let them rest for 5 minutes.

3. Apply some oil to the grill grate. Then, place the pineapple quarters on it and cover, further flipping them once the pieces are slightly charred after about 8 to 10 minutes. Transfer the pineapple to the serving platter.

4. Top with some coconut chips and drizzle with the remaining honey mixture.

9. Grilled Tofu Burgers with Lemon-Basil

Preparation Time: 20 min | Serving: 4 | Difficulty Level: Easy

Nutritional Info: Fat: 11.3g | Carbs: 34.5g | Protein: 10.5

Ingredients

- 1/3 cup chopped fresh basil
- 2 tbsp. Dijon mustard
- 2 tbsp. honey
- 2 tsp. grated lemon rind
- ¼ cup fresh lemon juice
- 1 tbsp. extra virgin olive oil
- ½ tsp. salt
- ¼ tsp. black pepper
- 4 garlic cloves, minced
- 1 lb. firm tofu, drained
- Cooking spray
- ⅓ cup kalamata olives, pitted and chopped
- 3 tbsp. sour cream
- 3 tbsp. light mayonnaise
- 6 hamburger buns
- 6 tomato slices
- 1 cup trimmed watercress

Steps for preparation

1. Place the first eight ingredients and 3 garlic cloves in a small bowl. Then, cut the tofu crosswise into six slices. Then, pat each square dry and place the tofu slices on the jelly roll pan. Then, brush both sides of the tofu slices with the lemon juice mixture and preserve the remaining juice mixture. Then, let the tofu stand for 1 hour.

2. Preheat the grill and coat it with some oil.

3. Place the tofu slices on the grill rack and grill for around 3 minutes on each side, brushing them with the leftover juice.

4. Then, in a small bowl, combine the remaining minced garlic clove, chopped olives, sour cream, and mayonnaise. Mix well and spread the mayonnaise over the bottom half of both hamburger buns. Then, add one tofu slice, tomato slice, two tablespoons of watercress, and the top half of the bun.

5. Serve and enjoy.

10. Grilled Peaches and Gingersnap Crumble

Preparation Time: 15 min | Serving: 4 | Difficulty Level: Easy

Nutritional Info: Fat: 9g | Carbs: 29g | Protein: 3g

Ingredients

- 1 tbsp. liquid cane sugar
- ½ tsp. ground cinnamon
- ½ tsp. ground ginger
- Canola oil
- 6 medium-sized fresh peaches, halved and pitted
- 1/3 cup heavy cream
- ½ tsp. vanilla extract
- 4 gingersnaps, roughly chopped
- 2 tbsp. fresh mint, sliced

Steps for preparation

1. Preheat the charcoal grill until it reaches the medium-high temperature of 400°F to 450°F. Then, mix together the cane sugar, cinnamon, and ginger in a small bowl. Brush the grill grates with some oil.

2. Place the peach halves on the grates and grill them until marks appear, which should take around 3 to 4 minutes. Flip the peaches and brush the tops with the sugar-cinnamon mixture. Continue grilling until the fruit become tender and the glaze begin to brown, which should take around 4 minutes. Remove them from the grill.

3. Beat the cream and vanilla until soft peaks form, for around 1 minute. Then, place three peach halves in four shallow bowls and mix them with the whipped cream.

4. Finally, top the mixture with the gingersnaps and mint. Serve immediately.

11. Perfect Grilled Zucchini

Preparation Time: 10 min | Serving: 4 | Difficulty Level: Easy

Nutritional Info: Fat: 3.5g | Carbs: 4g | Protein: 1g

Ingredients

- 2 medium-sized zucchini
- 1 tbsp. olive oil
- 1 tbsp. red wine vinegar
- 1 tsp. dried parsley
- 1 tsp. dried basil
- ½ tsp. garlic powder
- Kosher salt
- Black pepper

Steps for preparation

1. Preheat the grill until it reaches medium-high heat. Cut the zucchini into strips and put it in a large bowl. Then, add oil, parsley, basil, red wine vinegar, garlic powder, salt, and black pepper.

2. Place the zucchini on the grill and cook it for 2 to 3 minutes. Flip and continue cooking it on high heat while covered, for about 2 to 3 minutes. Remove from the heat.

3. Serve.

12. Grilled Garlic Broccoli

Preparation Time: 25 min | Serving: 4 | Difficulty Level: Easy

Nutritional Info: Fat: 7g | Carbs: 7g | Protein: 3g

Ingredients

- 4 cups broccoli florets
- 2 tbsp. olive oil
- ½ tsp. salt
- ½ tsp. black pepper
- ½ tsp. garlic powder
- ¼ tsp. red pepper flakes

Steps for preparation

1. Place the broccoli, salt, pepper, oil, and garlic powder in a bowl and mix, ensuring that the broccoli is seasoned well.

2. Then, place a large piece of foil on the grill. Put the broccoli on the foil and grill it for around 8 to 10 minutes until it gets slightly crisp.

3. Enjoy your broccoli!

13. Grilled Tofu with Spicy Peanut Sauce

Preparation Time: 10 min | Serving: 4 | Difficulty Level: Easy

Nutritional Info: Fat: 22g | Carbs: 12g | Protein: 14g

Ingredients

- 2 packs of tofu, drained
- Grapeseed oil
- 2 tbsp. light brown sugar
- ½ tsp. black pepper
- 1 tsp. salt
- ¼ cup of packed cilantro leaves
- 3 tbsp. salted peanuts
- 2 tbsp. olive oil
- 2 tbsp. toasted sesame oil
- 2 tbsp. rice vinegar
- 1 small garlic clove
- 1 red chili, seeded and chopped
- 2 tsp. fresh ginger, chopped
- 1 tsp. of fresh lime juice

Steps for preparation

1. Preheat the grill until it reaches around 450°F to 550°F. Then, cut the tofu in half in order to have four tofu strips. Wrap each strip in many layers of paper towels and leave them for 10 minutes.

2. Then, remove the paper towels and lightly brush the tofu with some grapeseed oil. Now, sprinkle some brown sugar, pepper, and salt over the tofu.

3. Pulse the remaining ingredients in the food processor.

4. Apply some grapeseed oil to the grill rack and grill the tofu until grill marks appear, for around 2 to 3 minutes per side. Then, cut each strip into three triangles.

5. Serve the tofu with some peanut sauce.

14. Grilled Vegetables Served with Creamy Turmeric Sauce.

Preparation Time: 25 min | Serving: 4 | Difficulty Level: Easy

Nutritional Info: Fat: 0g | Carbs: 0g | Protein: 0g

Ingredients

- 1/3 cup of whole-fat Greek yogurt
- 2 tbsp. of extra virgin olive oil
- ½ tsp. of ground turmeric
- 1 garlic clove, minced
- 2 tsp. lemon zest
- 1 tbsp. fresh lemon juice
- 1 tsp. salt
- 1 tsp. black pepper
- 1 large eggplant
- 1 large red bell pepper
- 1 large zucchini
- Grapeseed oil
- ¼ cup of pomegranate arils
- 3 tbsp. mint leaves

Steps for preparation

1. Preheat the grill to about medium-high heat (around 450°F). Mix the yogurt, turmeric, garlic, olive oil, lemon zest, lemon juice, and one tablespoon of water in a small bowl. Then, stir in some salt and black pepper.

2. Proceed to cut the eggplant lengthwise. Then, brush the bell pepper, yellow squash, zucchini, and eggplant with the grapeseed oil.

3. Now, generously apply grapeseed oil to the grill grate. Place the eggplant, zucchini, and yellow squash on the grill. Turn each piece once after around 10 minutes. Now, grill the bell pepper, while occasionally turning the pieces, for around 5 minutes.

4. Cut the eggplant diagonally into slices. Transfer the grilled vegetables to the platter and season with salt and black pepper. Finally, drizzle the sauce on the vegetables and sprinkle with pomegranate arils and mint.

5. Enjoy.

15. Grilled Tropical Fruit with Almond-Ricotta Sauce

Preparation Time: 10 min | Serving: 4 | Difficulty Level: Easy

Nutritional Info: Fat: 2g | Carbs: 1.3 | Protein: 4g

Ingredients

- ½ cup vanilla Greek yogurt
- ¼ cup of ricotta cheese
- 3 tbsp. packed brown sugar
- ¼ tsp. almond extract
- 1 fresh pineapple, peeled and cored
- 2 bananas, unpeeled
- Berries
- Coconut flakes

Steps for preparation

1. Combine the yogurt, brown sugar, ricotta cheese, and almond extract in a small bowl and stir well. Then, cover and chill in the refrigerator until it is to be served.

2. Clean the grill and spray some oil on the grates.

3. Preheat the grill until it reaches medium-high heat.

4. Lay the pineapple on the grill rack and close the lid. Turn the pineapple occasionally and wait until grill marks appear on each side, which should take about 8 to 10 minutes.

5. Place the unpeeled bananas on the grill and wait until sear marks appear.

6. Remove the fruit from the grill and serve with the almond-ricotta sauce, fresh berries, and coconut.

16. Grilled Avocado Stuffed with Chickpeas and Tahini

Preparation Time: 20 min | Serving: 4 | Difficulty Level: Easy

Nutritional Info: Fat: 14.2g | Carbs: 17.4g | Protein: 5.2g

Ingredients

- 1 can of chickpeas, drained
- Oil Spray
- ½ tsp. smoked paprika
- Salt and pepper
- 2 large avocados
- ½ cup cucumber, diced
- ½ cup cherry tomatoes
- 1½ tbsp. fresh lemon juice
- 2 tbsp. tahini
- Cilantro

Steps for preparation

1. Preheat the grill to medium-high heat.

2. Place the chickpeas in a small bowl and wait for them to dry. Then, spray them with grapeseed oil spray and add smoked paprika, salt, and pepper.

3. Place chickpeas in the bottom of the grill basket. Place on the grill and cook for around 10 minutes. Spray the chickpeas again with the grapeseed spray and stir. Then, cook for another ten minutes until they become crispy. Remove them from the heat and allow them to cool.

4. Cut the avocados in half and scoop out the seed. Spray some grapeseed oil on the avocados and season with salt and pepper. Place the fleshy-side down on the grill and allow it to grill until marks form, which should take about five minutes.

5. Mix the cucumber, tomatoes, and lemon juice in a small bowl and season with salt and pepper.

6. Divide the cucumber mixture into each of the avocado halves. Then, top each of the halves with one tablespoon of the prepared chickpeas. Drizzle with Tahini.

7. Serve and enjoy.

17. Grilled Sweet Potato Fries

Preparation Time: 5 min | Serving: 4 | Difficulty Level: Easy

Nutritional Info: Fat: 5g | Carbs: 19g | Protein: 1g

Ingredients

- 4 large sweet potatoes
- 2 tbsp. salt
- 2 tbsp. olive oil
- 1 tbsp. brown sugar
- 1 tsp. chipotle chili pepper
- French cilantro, chopped

Steps for preparation

1. Place the potatoes in a large pot of cold water. Add salt, bring to a boil, and allow the potatoes to cook until they are tender, for about 10 to 15 minutes.

2. Drain and let them cool slightly. Now, heat the grill until it reaches medium-high heat.

3. Slice the potatoes into wedges and peel off the skins. Place the wedges in a bowl and drizzle with olive oil. Season with some brown sugar, a teaspoon of salt, and chipotle chili pepper. Mix them together until the potatoes are evenly coated.

4. Grill the sweet potato fries for about 6 minutes until they become lightly golden. Remove the potatoes from the platter.

5. Serve.

Chapter 6: Grilled Salad Recipes

1. Grilled Snapper with Orzo Pasta Salad

Preparation Time: 20 min | Serving: 4 | Difficulty Level: Easy

Nutritional Info: Fat: 11.2g | Carbs: 39.3g | Protein: 32.7g

Ingredients

- 1½ cups uncooked orzo
- Cooking spray
- 4 6-oz. red snapper fillets
- ½ tsp. salt
- ¼ tsp. black pepper
- 1½ tbsp. shallots, minced
- 1 tbsp. fresh parsley, chopped
- 1 tbsp. fresh lemon juice
- 2 tsp. orange juice
- 1 tsp. Dijon mustard
- 2½ tbsp. extra virgin olive oil

Steps for preparation

1. Boil the pasta without any salt. Drain and keep warm.

2. Heat the grill pan over medium-high heat and coat it with cooking spray. Season the fish with salt and pepper and sauté it in the pan. Cook it for 3 minutes on both sides.

3. Combine the remaining salt, pepper, shallots, parsley, orange juice, lemon juice, and mustard in a small bowl. Stir well and slowly add the olive oil, while constantly stirring with the whisk. Drizzle the shallot mixture over the pasta and toss well until the pasta is evenly coated.

4. Serve immediately.

2. Grilled Romaine Salad

Preparation Time: 10 min | Serving: 4 | Difficulty Level: Easy

Nutritional Info: Fat: 4.3g | Carbs: 3g | Protein: 5g

Ingredients

- 2 heads romaine lettuce
- Olive oil (for brushing)
- ¾ cup quartered cherry tomatoes
- ½ cup of corn
- ½ cup crumbled goat cheese
- 1 avocado, sliced
- 2 tbsp. lemon juice, freshly squeezed
- 2 tbsp. red wine vinegar
- ¼ tsp. salt
- ½ tsp. Dijon mustard
- ¼ cup olive oil

Steps for preparation

1. Preheat the grill until it reaches medium-high heat. Brush the surface of the romaine lettuce leaves with some olive oil and grill for about 4-5 minutes, turning them occasionally. Then, place the lettuce leaves on the salad plate and top them with the tomatoes, avocado, corn, and goat cheese.

2. Drizzle the dressing over the food and serve.

   FOR THE DRESSING:

3. In a bowl, whisk together the red wine vinegar, lemon juice, salt, mustard, and olive oil.

3. Grilled Peaches with Yogurt and Brown Sugar

Preparation Time: 15 min | Serving: 4 | Difficulty Level: Easy

Nutritional Info: Fat: 3g | Carbs: 8.9g | Protein: 6g

Ingredients

- Two peaches

- 2 tsp. melted butter

- 2-4 tsp. brown sugar blend

- ¼ cup vanilla yogurt

Steps for preparation

1. Preheat the grill until it reaches medium-high heat. Cut the peaches in half and remove the pits.

2. Brush the peaches with some melted butter and place them skin-side down on the heated grill.

3. Cook them for 4 to 5 minutes and flip them over once they start becoming tender.

4. Sprinkle some of the brown sugar on the peaches.

5. Once the sugar caramelizes, remove from the grill and let them cool.

6. Serve immediately.

4. Grilled Sirloin Salad

Preparation Time: 20 min | Serving: 4 | Difficulty Level: Easy

Nutritional Info: Fat: 8.7g | Carbs: 22g | Protein: 30.4g

Ingredients

- 1 tbsp. chili powder

- 2 tsp. dried oregano

- 1 tsp. dried thyme

- ½ tsp. salt

- ½ tsp. onion powder

- ½ tsp. garlic powder

- ¼ tsp. black pepper

- Sirloin steak, trimmed

- 8 cups of salad greens

- 1½ cups red bell pepper, cut into strips

- 1 cup red onion, sliced

- 1 tbsp. fresh parsley, chopped

- 1 tbsp. red wine vinegar

- 1 tsp. olive oil

- 1 tsp. fresh lemon juice

- 1 can whole-kernel corn, drained and rinsed

Steps for preparation

1. Combine the first seven ingredients together. Then, proceed to rub the spices onto the sides of the steak. Heat the nonstick grill pan over medium-high heat.

2. Then, place the steak on the pan and cook for 5 minutes on each side or until the meat reaches the desired degree of doneness. Cut the steak across the grain into thin slices.

3. While the steak cooks, combine the salad greens and remaining ingredients in a large bowl. Toss well to coat. Then, top with the steak and serve.

5. Chicken Teriyaki Drumsticks with the Tropical Fruit Salad

Preparation Time: 25 min | Serving: 4 | Difficulty Level: Easy

Nutritional Info: Fat: 9g | Carbs: 25g | Protein: 40g

Ingredients

- ¼ cup pineapple juice
- 3 tbsp. soy sauce
- 1 tbsp. light brown sugar
- 2 tsp. cornstarch
- Cooking spray
- 8 chicken drumsticks, skinned
- ¾ tsp. black pepper
- 1 cup fresh pineapple chunks
- 1 cup kiwi, peeled and sliced
- 1 cup halved fresh strawberries
- 1 tbsp. fresh cilantro, chopped
- 2 tbsp. lime juice
- ½ tsp. fresh ginger, peeled

Steps for preparation

1. In a shallow saucepan, whisk together the pineapple juice, brown sugar, soy sauce, and cornstarch over medium heat and wait for it to simmer. Then, cook it for 30 seconds, continuously stirring with a fork. Remove from the heat.

2. Place a grill pan over a medium-high flame and apply some cooking spray to it. Brush some oil on the chicken and sprinkle half a teaspoon of pepper over it. Place the chicken in the pan and cook it for 8 minutes, sometimes turning it over. Lower the heat and pour in some soy sauce. Allow the food to simmer for 15

minutes or until it is cooked, rotating and then brushing with the soy sauce mixture.

3. In a bowl, mix the remaining pepper, pineapple bits, strawberries, kiwi, cilantro, and ginger. Serve with the chicken and eat.

6. Grilled Cantaloupe Salad with Feta Cheese

Preparation Time: 15 min | Serving: 6 | Difficulty Level: Easy

Nutritional Info: Fat: 29g | Carbs: 18g | Protein: 9g

Ingredients

- 1 small shallot, diced
- 5 tbsp. champagne vinegar
- 1 tsp. honey
- 1½ tsp. salt
- Black pepper, to taste
- 5 tbsp. olive oil
- 1 cantaloupe, diced
- 1 English cucumber, sliced
- 6 oz. feta cheese, crumbled
- 3 oz. watercress
- 1 cup toasted hazelnuts, chopped

Steps for preparation

1. Preheat the grill until it reaches a high temperature of 500°F. Place the shallot and vinegar in a small bowl, allowing it to sit for 5 minutes. Now stir in the honey, salt, pepper, and oil.

2. Mix the cantaloupe and the remaining 1 tablespoon of oil in the large bowl. Place the cantaloupe on the oiled grates and allow it to roast uncovered until the grill marks appear, which should take around 2 to 3 minutes per side.

3. Transfer the grilled cantaloupe to the serving platter. Top it with some cucumber slices, feta cheese, and hazelnuts. Drizzle it with some vinaigrette and sprinkle the remaining salt on top.

4. Serve and enjoy.

7. Grilled Lamb Skewers with Warm Fava Bean Salad

Preparation Time: 15 min | Serving: 2 | Difficulty Level: Easy

Nutritional Info: Fat: 10.3g | Carbs: 23g | Protein: 24.8g

Ingredients

- 4 cups fava beans
- 1½ tsp. extra virgin olive oil
- 1 tbsp. fresh mint, chopped
- 1 tsp. grated lemon rind
- 2 tbsp. fresh lemon juice
- 1 tsp. salt
- ½ tsp. black pepper
- 2 tbsp. water
- 1½ lb. lamb leg, trimmed and cut into 1-inch cubes.
- Cooking spray
- 6 lemon wedges

Steps for preparation

1. Place some water in a pot and allow it to boil. Once it boils, pour the fava beans in the water for around 1 minute or until it gets tender. Then, drain the beans and rinse them with some cold water before draining once again. Remove the tough outer skin from the beans and discard the skins.

2. Combine and whisk together the olive oil, mint, lemon rind, lemon juice, salt, and black pepper in a medium-sized bowl. Heat 2 tablespoons of water in a saucepan over medium-high heat and add the beans to the pan. Cook them for 2 minutes or until the beans are completely hot. Now, add the beans to the juice mixture and toss them to coat.

3. Preheat the grill and apply some cooking spray to it.

4. Thread the lamb cubes onto skewers and spray them with cooking oil. Season the skewers evenly with the remaining salt and pepper. Place the skewers on the grill rack with the cooking spray and grill them for 7 minutes until the lamb is done. Continue to rotate them on occasion.

5. Serve with salad and lemon wedges.

8. Grilled Vegetable and Flank Steak Salad with Cheese Vinaigrette

Preparation Time: 30 min | Serving: 4 | Difficulty Level: Easy

Nutritional Info: Fat: 22.2g | Carbs: 8g | Protein: 28g

Ingredients

- 1 1 lb. flank steak, trimmed
- ¼ cup olive oil
- ½ tsp. garlic powder
- ¾ tsp. salt
- ½ tsp. black pepper
- 2 medium-sized yellow squash, halved lengthwise
- 2 ½-inch-thick red onion slices
- 1 red bell pepper, quartered
- 1½ tbsp. white wine vinegar
- Sugar
- 1 oz. blue cheese, crumbled
- ½ cup halved grape tomatoes

Steps for preparation

1. Warm the grill until it reaches medium-high heat.
2. Add garlic powder, oil, salt, and a pinch of pepper to the meat. Proceed to coat the steak with oil and place it in a pan. Cook the meat on either side for 4 minutes before removing and placing it on a cutting board.
3. Allow it to rest and then cut it.
4. Serve immediately.

Chapter 7: Miscellaneous

1. Grilled Herb and Cheese Stuffed Mushrooms

Preparation Time: 15 min | Serving: 4 | Difficulty Level: Easy

Nutritional Info: Fat: 12g | Carbs: 23g | Protein: 8g

Ingredients

- 4 large Portobello mushrooms
- ¼ cup panko breadcrumbs
- 1 tbsp. thyme, finely chopped
- 1 tbsp. oregano, finely chopped
- 2 tsp. rosemary, finely chopped
- 1 clove garlic, minced
- Salt
- Black pepper
- 1 oz. pimentos, chopped
- 1 tbsp. olive oil
- 2 tbsp. butter
- ¼ cup cheddar cheese (grated)

Steps for preparation

1. Wash the mushrooms and cut off the stems. Reserve the caps and finely chop the stems.
2. Mix together the breadcrumbs, thyme, oregano, rosemary, mushroom stems, garlic, salt, and pepper.
3. Pulse the mixture 15 times in the processor.
4. Stir in the pimentos.
5. Preheat the grill on medium-high heat and add some oil to the grill.
6. Brush the mushroom caps with olive oil and add 1/2 a teaspoon of butter to the inside of the cap.
7. Place the mushroom caps on the grill for 4 minutes.

8. Remove them from the grill, stuff with the breadcrumb mixture, and top with the grated cheese.

9. Return the mushroom caps to the grill and cook them for 4 minutes.

10. Remove them from the heat and allow them to rest for 5 minutes. Cut them into pieces and serve.

2. Grilled Portobello-Goat Cheese Pitas

Preparation Time: 15 min | Serving: 4 | Difficulty Level: Easy

Nutritional Info: Fat: 8.5g | Carbs: 39.8g | Protein: 11.9g

Ingredients

- 1 ½ tsp. garlic, minced
- 1 tsp. olive oil
- 4 6-inch pita pieces
- ½ tsp. salt
- ¼ tsp. black pepper
- 1 package of Portobello mushrooms
- Medium tomatoes, thick slices
- 1/3 cup goat cheese
- ½ cup fresh basil, chopped

Steps for preparation

1. Preheat the grill pan to medium-high heat.

2. Then, combine the garlic and oil and brush the mixture evenly over the pita bread pieces. Sprinkle a pinch of salt and pepper on the bread and place them in a pan to toast lightly.

3. Sprinkle a bit of salt and pepper evenly on the mushrooms and tomatoes. Place the mushrooms in the pan and cook them for 6 minutes or until they are tender, stirring them once. Remove the mushrooms from the pan and add the tomatoes, allowing them to cook for 1 minute.

4. Spread the goat cheese evenly on the pitas, then add the mushrooms and tomatoes. Finally, top with the chopped basil.

5. Serve.

Conclusion

After completing this book and trying out many of the recipes, your skills will continue to improve and you will no longer remain a novice griller. You must continue practicing your grilling skills to ensure that they continue to improve so that you can eventually become a grilling expert!

Recipe Name

Preparation Time:

Serving:

Difficulty Level:

Ingredients

_____

_____

_____

_____

_____

Steps for preparation

_____

_____

_____

_____

_____

_____

_____

_____

_____

_____

_____

_____

_____

Recipe Name

Preparation Time:

Serving:

Difficulty Level:

Ingredients

_____

_____

_____

_____

_____

Steps for preparation

_____

_____

_____

_____

_____

_____

_____

_____

_____

_____

_____

Recipe Name

Preparation Time:

Serving:

Difficulty Level:

Ingredients

_____

_____

_____

_____

_____

Steps for preparation

_____

_____

_____

_____

_____

_____

_____

_____

_____

_____

_____

_____

Recipe Name

Preparation Time:

Serving:

Difficulty Level:

Ingredients

_____

_____

_____

_____

_____

Steps for preparation

_____

_____

_____

_____

_____

_____

_____

_____

_____

_____

_____

Recipe Name

Preparation Time:

Serving:

Difficulty Level:

Ingredients

_____

_____

_____

_____

_____

Steps for preparation

_____

_____

_____

_____

_____

_____

_____

_____

_____

_____

_____

Recipe Name

Preparation Time:

Serving:

Difficulty Level:

Ingredients

_____

_____

_____

_____

_____

Steps for preparation

_____

_____

_____

_____

_____

_____

_____

_____

_____

_____

_____

Recipe Name

Preparation Time:

Serving:

Difficulty Level:

Ingredients

_____

_____

_____

_____

_____

Steps for preparation

_____

_____

_____

_____

_____

_____

_____

_____

_____

_____

_____

_____